BURNT L

Cover art by Lena Espinoza.
Illustrations by Lena Espinoza.

Printed in the United States of America.

First printing, 2020.

To Frankie.
You will forever live on in my
memory.

crush

it's the eyes that sparkle
just to spite me

your infuriating jawline
and fucking stupid hands
that would fit mine so perfectly

lips so frustrating
I want to bite them until they bleed

and make you understand how painful it is

to love another

stuck

nothing in the way you carded your fingers through your
hair
gave way to the emotions inside the broad of your shoulders

knocking the breath out

leaving the mind with nothing but doubts

I showed you the worst of me
and you stayed
with no idea of what you've done

those nights stuck like glue

sunday

soft sighs filling the room
silk sheets refusing to bloom

sun gleaming through
swollen eyes come into view

sunday mornings, spent with you

seven wonders

and not even the seven wonders of the world
could fascinate me as much as your fingertips

lingering on bleach white bed sheets

the last words spinning around in my head
like some sort of twister

legs as long as summer days
eyes that shield the reasons we couldn't keep it together

not even the seven wonders

lovely

I can feel the sleep creeping its way into my bones

the weight of my eyes and terrible decisions

letting you get to me was my biggest mistake

and you are lovely in ways I can't explain

we are we

feathered lashes on cheeks
curtains disclosing orbs of the crescent sea
limbs entangled, we are we

sifting from one minute to the next
fingers dashing across solid flesh
upon your shoulder, I rest

heavy sheets encasing our bodies
comfort in the blackest of night
companionship with no end in sight

a smile, that which fills me with hope
there's a light I can finally see
hands intertwined, we are we

finally

I feel as though
we've been together
from the moment time began

slurred words and moonlit hours
bare chests pressed so tight
heartbeats steadily syncing
instead of the sinking she was so used to

she sees colors again
the translucent purple of a sunset

she was finally able
to go home

together

it was when we were resting skin to skin

the ink embedded in the pages coming alive underneath your
tongue

just like I did

ebb and flow

arousal coils in the pit of my stomach

your scent drenching my sheets

bodies ebbing and flowing
like the sea taken hostage by a storm

symphonies sounding off
a reflection of your fears in the dark

identity tossed alongside your clothes
you are the focal point

never

I don't wanna think about how
my big pants don't fit me anymore
I don't wanna think at all

I want you to do the thinking for me
to plant those seeds that will magically make me think
I'm beautiful

but I've never been beautiful
not when I was being forced
to do things I didn't want to
and not when I was loved

especially not now
locked inside the bathroom
trying to be quiet
so no one hears me crying

I will never be beautiful
not even when you love me

you

I love you
I've loved you since the first day
I heard your voice

I trust you
giving me butterflies
and gold plated promises

I envy you
unbroken heart and genuine smiles
you grew up safe

I lost you
foreign and estranged although
our breaths mingle

I hate you
left behind in the collapse
wishing I was deaf

alone

I wake up in the morning
alone

I brush my teeth
and in my reflection
I see you

your shampoo in the corner
your scent on my bed

visions of you
laughing on the porch

your bitter words
in my coffee

your clothes in our closet
my closet

cigarette butts
with your lipstick stains

the ghost of your mouth
as I cook

I go to bed
alone

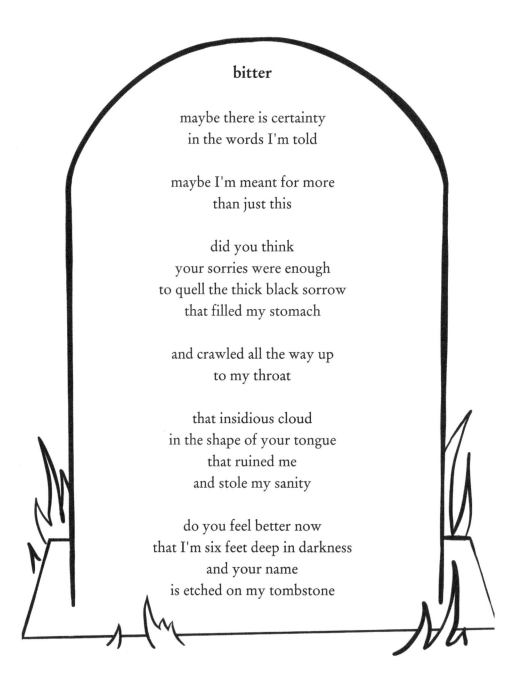

bitter

maybe there is certainty
in the words I'm told

maybe I'm meant for more
than just this

did you think
your sorries were enough
to quell the thick black sorrow
that filled my stomach

and crawled all the way up
to my throat

that insidious cloud
in the shape of your tongue
that ruined me
and stole my sanity

do you feel better now
that I'm six feet deep in darkness
and your name
is etched on my tombstone

nothing

one o' clock
and all I can feel
is regret for letting you in

filling me with butterflies
only to set them ablaze

letting your nails
rake into my heart
flooding its chambers with confusion

and aren't I the fool
to crave your arms
your stunning whispers

and then nothing

you let me feel

nothing

anew

weaving the threads
cutting my thumb
on the thimble

turning the soil
to plant anew

I am for myself
I am no longer
for you

strangers

I talk to strangers on the internet
because they don't know my father used to hit me

they don't know the colors of my niece's eyes
or what it felt like to hear that your brother didn't make it

and most of all
they can't see the scars on my skin
or my google search history of free online therapy
because my mother can't afford it

I post a selfie with a hashtag
and many or no people "like" it
because many or no people like me

I don't like me

but they can't possibly know that
because I try very hard to mask it
with my humor and pretty words

status update after status update
scrolling and scrolling
until I find out that my own sister
didn't even post on my wall for my birthday

not that it matters

not that anything matters

someday I'll be an in memoriam page
and maybe everyone
or maybe no one
will pay their respects

except for those strangers I once spoke to on the internet

INDEX

ACKNOWLEDGMENTS

I want to thank my lovely little sister, Lena, for providing the artwork in this book, and for continuing to be the best friend I have ever had. I thank Annie O'Sullivan for her knowledge and guidance when it comes to formatting and editing. I thank my lovely family for all of their love and inspiration. I can only hope I offended none of you. I thank my friends for their unending support and belief in me. None of this is possible without each and every one of you being there for me every step of the way. I thank my partner, Joseph, for his love. I thank Frankie for absolutely everything. Now this date will have a new meaning. I truly thank anyone who has ever read one bit of my poetry, anyone that has ever praised it, and anyone that has ever criticized it.

And, most importantly, I thank myself for never giving up on me.

CPSIA information can be obtained
at www.ICGtesting.com
Printed in the USA
LVHW031132040720
659733LV00002B/179